Reading American History

Quakers in Early America

Written by Melinda Lilly
Illustrated by Yohanis Díaz

Educational Consultants
Kimberly Weiner, Ed.D
Betty Carter, Ed.D

Rourke
Publishing LLC
Vero Beach, Florida 32963

www.rourkepublishing.com

A Migue por hacer de esta historia algo maravilloso.
To Migue for making this story something special.
—Y. D.

Designer: Elizabeth J. Bender

Art Direction: Rigo Aguirre, www.versalgroup.com

Library of Congress Cataloging-in-Publication Data

Lilly, Melinda.
  Quakers in early America / Melinda Lilly; illustrated by Yohanis Díaz.
    p. cm. — (Reading American history)
  Summary: A simple introduction to William Penn, the Quakers, and their life in colonial Pennsylvania.
  ISBN 1-58952-370-9
  1. Quakers—United States—History—Juvenile literature. 2. Quakers—Pennsylvania—History—Juvenile literature. 3. Penn, William, 1644-1718—Juvenile literature. 4. United States—History—Colonial period, ca. 1600-1775—Juvenile literature. 5. Pennsylvania—History—Colonial period, ca. 1600-1775—Juvenile literature. [1. Quakers. 2. Penn, William, 1644-1718. 3. Pennsylvania—History—Colonial period, ca. 1600-1775.] I. Díaz, illus. II. Title.

E184.F89 L45 2002
974.8'0088286—dc21   2002017847

Cover Illustration: William and Hannah Penn with the Liberty Bell, in front of a depiction of early Pennsylvania

Time Line

Help students follow this story by introducing important events in the Time Line.

1681   William Penn receives the charter
        for Pennsylvania.

1701   Charter of Privileges is adopted.

1718   William Penn dies.

1751   Pennsylvania Assembly orders the Liberty Bell.

1776   Liberty Bell rings to celebrate the reading of
        the Declaration of Independence.

1783   Revolutionary War ends.

1788   U. S. Constitution ratified.

The **Quakers** wanted freedom to practice their **religion**. They came to America.

The Quakers come to America by ship.

In America, others still punished them for their beliefs.

Puritans punish a Quaker for practicing her religion.

William Penn was a Quaker. In 1681, he convinced the king of England to give him land in America. The king gave him **Pennsylvania**.

The king and William Penn

In Pennsylvania, the Quakers shared their freedom. They thought all people had a right to their beliefs.

Quakers meet with people of other religions.

The Quakers thought war was wrong. The Quakers and the **Native Americans** lived in peace.

Quakers and Native Americans

The Quakers wanted laws written to protect their freedom. They asked William Penn to write them.

Asking William Penn, in front of his home

In 1701, William Penn wrote the **Charter of Privileges**. He based it on Quaker ideas of freedom. It helped lead to the U. S. **Constitution**.

William Penn writes.

Fifty years later, the **Liberty Bell** was made. It honors the Charter of Privileges.

The Liberty Bell in Pennsylvania

Today, Quakers still live by those ideas of freedom.

Going to a Quaker meeting

21

Word List

Charter of Privileges (CHAR ter OV PRIV uh lij ez)—Written by William Penn in 1701, the Charter of Privileges protected the religious freedom of the people of Pennsylvania and granted some governmental powers to its Assembly.

Constitution (kon stih TOO shun)—The main laws of the U. S.

Liberty Bell (LIB er tee BEL)—A symbol of the U. S., it hangs in Liberty Hall, Philadelphia.

Native Americans (NAY tiv uh MER ih kunz)—Members of the peoples native to North America; American Indians

Pennsylvania (pen sil VANE yuh)—An eastern state in the U. S.

Penn, William (PEN, WIL yum)—The Quaker founder of Pennsylvania

Puritans (PYOOR ih tunz)—Members of the Puritan faith, a strict Christian religion

Quakers (KWAY kerz)—Members of the Religious Society of Friends, a Christian religion

religion (rih LIJ un)—Beliefs about the fundamental questions of life; faith

Books to Read

Benge, Janet, and Geoff Benge. *William Penn: Liberty and Justice for All*. Emerald Books, 2002.

Blanc, Felice. *I Am a Quaker*. PowerKids, 1999.

Stefoff, Rebecca, and Sandra Stotsky. *William Penn*. Chelsea House, 2000.

Wister, Sally. *A Colonial Quaker Girl: The Diary of Sally Wister, 1777–1778*. Suzanne L. Bunkers, Megan O'Hara, editors. Blue Earth Books, 2000.

Websites to Visit

www.dep.state.pa.us/dep/PA_Env-Her/William_Penn.htm

www.pym.org/exhibit/p078.html

www.pym.org/exhibit/p045.html

www.ushistory.org/libertybell/

www.amphilsoc.org/library/exhibits/treasures/charter.htm

Index